KINGFISHER
READERS

level
2

Birds
of Prey

Claire Llewellyn

 KINGFISHER

First published 2017 by Kingfisher
an imprint of Macmillan Children's Books
20 New Wharf Road, London N1 9RR
Associated companies throughout the world
www.panmacmillan.com

Series editor: Hayley Down
Literacy consultant: Hilary Horton
Design: Peter Clayman

ISBN 978-0-7534-4094-0

9 8 7 6 5 4 3 2 1

1TR/0317/WKT/UG/105MA

A CIP catalogue record for this book is available from the British Library.

Printed in China

Picture credits
The Publisher would like to thank the following for permission to reproduce their material.
Top = t; Bottom = b; Centre = c; Left = l; Right = r
Cover iStock/Kandfoto; Pages 4–5 iStock/Dgwildlife; 5t Shutterstock/Dennis W Donohue; 6 Shutterstock/
Glass and Nature; 6–7 iStock/Byrdyak; 7 Shutterstock/Martin-Kubik; 8 Shutterstock/Alexey Stiop; 9t iStock/
MonteComeau, 9m iStock/James Pintar; 10–11 Shutterstock/Keneva Photography; 12 iStock/Lakes4life; 13t
flpa/Photo Researchers, 13b iStock/Mark-paton; 14 iStock/cadifor, 14–15 iStock/Holcy; 15 Nature Picture
Library/Nick Garbutt; 16–17 Getty/Minden Pictures; 17 iStock/kajornyot; 18 iStock/jimkruger, 18–19 iStock/
cnmacdon; 20, 21t, 21b iStock/Bousfield; 22t iStock/Anagramm, 22–23 iStock/ottoduplessis; 24 Getty/
PREAU Louis-Marie/hemis.fr; 25t iStock/Lokibaho, 25b Shutterstock/Juha Saastamoinen; 26 Getty/Auscape/
Contributor; 27 Getty/Wayne Lynch; 28b iStock/ Brian Balster, 28–29 iStock/fotokostic; 29t iStock/ozflash; 30
iStock/Beka_C; 31t iStock/mzphoto11, 31b Shutterstock/Katiekk.

Contents

What are birds of prey?

Birds of **prey** are powerful birds with sharp claws and a hooked beak. These birds hunt for food.

They spot animals on the ground, and fly down to kill them with their claws. Then they rip off the meat with their beak.

white-tailed sea eagle

All kinds of birds

There are about 450 kinds of birds of prey. Scientists sort them into groups, such as eagles, vultures, falcons or owls. Can you see some of the differences between these birds?

kestrel

boreal owl

Eagles and vultures
are the biggest birds.
Falcons are smaller and
faster. Owls are the only
birds that hunt at night.

vulture

Let's find them!

Birds of prey live all over the world in many different **habitats**.

desert eagle
owl

They live in deserts, **grasslands** and rainforests.

They live by lakes, rivers and coasts.

osprey

snowy owl

They live in mountains, cold forests and the icy Arctic.

The only places birds of prey do not live are Antarctica and the oceans far from land.

The body of a hunter

A bird of prey's body is built for hunting.

Long, sharp claws called **talons** stab the prey and grip it tightly.

Sharp eyes
spot prey
down below.

Hooked beak
tears off the meat.

Strong wings
lift the bird of prey
high into the air.

red-tailed kite

Danger in the sky

A kestrel is a kind of falcon.
It **hovers** in the air to look for prey.
It flaps its wings very quickly to
stay in the same place.

kestrel

peregrine falcon

The peregrine falcon catches birds in mid-air. When it spots a bird flying below, it folds back its wings, dives like an arrow and grabs its prey.

What do they eat?

Different birds of prey feed on different animals. Many birds feed on rabbits, mice and voles. Some feed on lizards and snakes.

common buzzard

Other birds of prey catch snails, crabs and fish.

red-tailed hawk

harpy
eagle

The powerful harpy eagle
lives in the rainforests of
South America. It snatches
monkeys from the treetops.

barn owl

Night hunters

Owls are night hunters. They fly silently. They have softer feathers than other birds so their prey does not hear them coming.

pygmy owl

Owls see well with their large eyes.
They hear well with the big ear
holes on the sides of their head.
They can even hear the tiny
sounds of animals on the ground.

Snowy owls

The snowy owl's thick white feathers keep it warm in the Arctic.

They also blend in well with the snow, hiding the bird as it hunts for hares.

The snowy owl hunts **lemmings**, too. Lemmings live in underground tunnels. The owl can't see them, but it can hear them! It dives to catch them through the snow.

Fishing birds

Some birds of prey are good at fishing. When an osprey spots a fish, it dives into the water. Its talons grab the slippery prey, and hold it tight.

The osprey is dripping wet but its strong wings beat hard. They lift the bird and its catch back into the air.

Vultures

Vultures don't kill
their food. They feed
on animals that are
already dead. A group
of vultures will spread
out in the sky until one
of them spots a meal.

The vultures feed on the rotting **carcass**. It is very mucky work! The birds have no feathers on their head and so they stay fairly clean.

Nesting time

Birds of prey build their nests in the spring. Some nest in trees; others choose rocky ledges or nest on the ground. Many return with the same **mate** to the same nest every year.

eagle owl chicks

great horned owl

The female bird lays the eggs and sits on them for up to eight weeks.

osprey

The male hunts for food and keeps other birds away.

Growing up

When the chicks **hatch** out of their egg, they are covered with soft fluffy **down**. They cannot fly or hunt for food. Their parents feed them strips of meat so they grow very fast.

kestrel chick

A bird must grow strong feathers before it learns to fly. This is called **fledging**. The birds must also learn to hunt or they will starve. Most young birds leave home before they are five months old.

great grey owl
and chick

Birds in danger

All around the world, birds of prey are losing their habitats. This is because people are chopping down forests and clearing land for building and farms. Every type of bird needs its habitat; it cannot live anywhere else.

Farming can harm birds. Many farmers spray their crops to poison insects and other animals. When birds of prey eat these animals, they get sick too.

barn owl

Protecting birds

Some types of birds are now very rare. They could die out and become **extinct**. Scientists are helping to protect them in different ways.

They **breed** chicks in safe places and set them free in the wild.

vulture chick

Many people are trying to
protect habitats and stop others
from chopping down trees.
They are also setting
up parks and reserves
where birds of prey
will be safe.

golden
eagle

Glossary

breed to keep animals and help them have babies

carcass the dead body of an animal

down fine soft feathers

extinct when an animal or plant has died out completely

fledging growing feathers strong enough to fly

grasslands dry, open grassy areas

habitat the kind of place where an animal lives

hatch to break out of an egg

hover to flap the wings quickly so as to stay in one place

lemming a small animal that lives in tunnels

mate an animal that has young with another

prey an animal hunted and killed for food

talons the hooked claws of a bird